Awesome Rocks

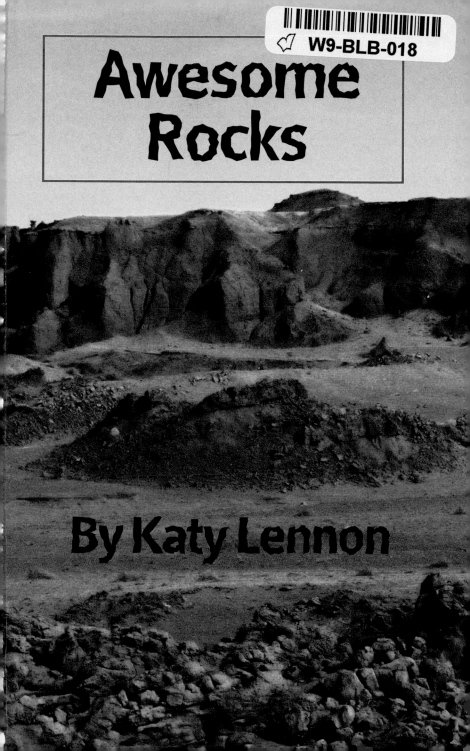

By Katy Lennon

Penguin
Random
House

Series Editor Deborah Lock
US Senior Editor Shannon Beatty
Editors Pomona Zaheer, Arpita Nath
Project Editor Camilla Gersh
Editor Katy Lennon
Designer Emma Hobson
Art Editor Jyotsna Julka
Managing Editor Soma B. Chowdhury
Managing Art Editor Ahlawat Gunjan
Art Director Martin Wilson

Senior Producer, Pre-production Ben Marcus
Illustrator Emma Hobson
DTP Designers Anita Yadav,
Nityanand Kumar
Picture Researcher Surya Sankash Sarangi,
Aditya Katyal

Reading Consultant
Dr. Linda Gambrell, Ph.D.
Subject Consultant
Kevin Walsh

First American Edition, 2015
Published in the United States by DK Publishing
345 Hudson Street, New York, New York 10014

Copyright © 2015 Dorling Kindersley Limited
A Penguin Random House Company.
15 16 17 18 19 10 9 8 7 6 5 4 3 2 1
001—275326—September/15

A catalog record for this book is available from the Library of Congress.
ISBN: 978-1-4654-3563-7 (pb)
ISBN: 978-1-4654-3562-0 (hc)

DK books are available at special discounts when purchased in bulk for sales promotions,
premiums, fund-raising, or educational use.
For details, contact: DK Publishing Special Markets,
345 Hudson Street, New York, New York 10014 or SpecialSales@dk.com.

Printed and bound in China

The publisher would like to thank the following for their kind permission to reproduce their photographs:
(Key: a-above; b-below/bottom; c-center ; f-far; l-left; r-right; t-top; OUM- Oxford University Museum of Natural History;
NHM- The Natural History Museum, London)
1 Corbis: Louie Psihoyos. **4 Dorling Kindersley:** OUM (t/b); **Pearson Asset Library:** Coleman Yuen (ca/Brush) NHM (Top and Bottom Grid). **Dreamstime.com:** Humbak (t/b) Also appears on 4,6,8,10,12,22,24,26,28,30,36,38,40,42,44,50,52,54,56,58,66,68,70,7 2,74,84,86,88,90,92,102,104,106,108,110,112,122,124,126. **5 Dorling Kindersley:** NHM (t/b). **Dreamstime.com:** Humbak (tl, tc) Also appears on 5,7,9,11,13,23,25,27,29,31,37,39,41,43,45,51,53,55,57,59,67,69,71,73,75,85,87,89,91,93,103,105,107,109,111,113,12 3,125,127. **10-11 Dorling Kindersley:** OUM. **12 Dorling Kindersley:** NHM. **14 Dorling Kindersley:** OUM(bl). **15 Dorling Kindersley:** NHM (cr, br). **16 Dorling Kindersley:** OUM (bl); NHM (c). **17 Dorling Kindersley:** NHM (cl, br, r, bl). **18 Dorling Kindersley:** OUM (bl). **19 Dorling Kindersley:** NHM (cr, br). **20 Dorling Kindersley:** OUM (bl); NHM (clb, clb/Obsidian). **Fotolia:** John Takai (tc). **21 Dorling Kindersley:** NHM (cr, cla); The Museum of London (clb). **22 Dorling Kindersley:** NHM (ca). **31 Dorling Kindersley:** NHM (br). **32 Alamy Images:** Realimage (br). **Dorling Kindersley:** OUM (bl); Whipple Museum of History of Science, Cambridge (c). **33 Alamy Images:** Michele and Tom Grimm (crb). **Dorling Kindersley:** NHM (cr). **34 Dorling Kindersley:** OUM (bl). **35 Dorling Kindersley:** NHM (cr). **36 Dorling Kindersley:** NHM (cla). **41 Dorling Kindersley:** NHM. **44 Getty Images:** Mint Images / Frans Lanting (c). **46 Dorling Kindersley:** OUM (bl). **46-47 Getty Images:** National Geographic / Herbert S. Wilburn Jr.. **47 Dorling Kindersley:** NHM (cr). **48 Dorling Kindersley:** OUM (bl). **49 Dorling Kindersley:** NHM (cr, br). **50 Dorling Kindersley:** NHM (cra). **53 Alamy Images:** Jupiterimages (c). **60 Dorling Kindersley:** NASA (cla); OUM (bl). **61 Dorling Kindersley:** NHM (cr, br). **62 Dorling Kindersley:** OUM (bl); NHM (cr). **63 Dorling Kindersley:** NHM (cr, br). **64 Dorling Kindersley:** OUM (bl); NHM (br). **65 Dorling Kindersley:** NHM (cr, br, fcl, cl, c, fcr, bl, bc, br/Monoclinic Crystal). **66 Dorling Kindersley:** The Science Museum, London (cla/Scheelite). **68 Getty Images:** Mint Images / Frans Lanting (c); Oliver Strewe (b). **70 Dorling Kindersley:** The Science Museum, London (bl). **71 Dorling Kindersley:** Company Audiotel (r). **76 Dorling Kindersley:** OUM (bl). **Fotolia:** Valdis Torms (b). **77 Dorling Kindersley:** NHM (cr, br). **78 Dorling Kindersley:** OUM (bl). **79 Dorling Kindersley:** NHM (cr, br). **80 Dorling Kindersley:** OUM (fbl); NHM (bl). **81 Dorling Kindersley:** NHM (cr, br). **82 Dorling Kindersley:** OUM(bl). **83 Dorling Kindersley:** NHM (cr, br). **89 Dorling Kindersley:** NHM. **93 Dorling Kindersley:** OUM. **94 Dorling Kindersley:** OUM (bl). **95 Dorling Kindersley:** NHM (cr, br). **96 Dorling Kindersley:** OUM (bl). **97 Dorling Kindersley:** NHM (cr, br). **98 Dorling Kindersley:** OUM (bl); NHM (clb, bc). **99 Dorling Kindersley:** NHM (cr, br, crb, bl). **100 Dorling Kindersley:** OUM (bl). **101 Dorling Kindersley:** NHM (cr, br, bl). **104 Dorling Kindersley:** NHM. **106 Dorling Kindersley:** OUM. **109 Dorling Kindersley:** NHM. **113 Dorling Kindersley:** NHM. **114-115 Alamy Images:** Hilary Morgan (c). **114 Corbis:** Francis G. Mayer (br). **Dorling Kindersley:** OUM (bl). **115 Alamy Images:** Marc Tielemans (cra/jewellery display box). **Corbis:** Fred Ward (br); Reuters (cf/Diamond). **Dorling Kindersley:** NHM (cr, fbr). **116 Dorling Kindersley:** OUM (bl); NHM (c). **117 Dorling Kindersley:** NHM (cr, br). **118 Dorling Kindersley:** OUM (bl). **119 Dorling Kindersley:** NHM (cr, br). **120 Dorling Kindersley:** OUM (bl). **121 Alamy Images:** imageBROKER. **Dorling Kindersley:** NHM (cr, br) **Jacket images:** Back: **Dorling Kindersley:** NHM ftl, cra. Spine: **Dorling Kindersley:** NHM
All other images © Dorling Kindersley
For further information see: www.dkimages.com

A WORLD OF IDEAS:
SEE ALL THERE IS TO KNOW

www.dk.com

CONTENTS

CHAPTER 1

GEOLOGY ROCKS!

Rocks and minerals are the building blocks of our planet—without them we would have nothing to stand on but thin air! From a tiny pebble on the beach to a giant boulder in the desert, every rock has an exciting story to tell. Stone-sleuthing scientists work to unearth these stories and learn about our planet—they are called geologists.

Geology is the study of the Earth and all the natural materials within it. Enthusiastic geologists follow crumbled clues to dig up

information about life on Earth. Rocks and minerals can tell us a lot about what the Earth was like in the past and this knowledge helps scientists predict what might happen in the future. Geologists sniff out evidence of past earthquakes, floods, and volcanic eruptions from the ground below us so they can build up a picture of the Earth's life. They can even gather information about the animals that walked the Earth millions of years ago from one tiny fossil!

The quest for rocks, minerals, and fossils takes geologists on great adventures across the globe, and even beyond. Rocks are formed in many far-flung locations, not just on Earth but out in space too! It is a geologist's job to find and understand each of these rocks and unlock the mysteries from within them.

Earth is made of layers, just like a giant onion. At the very center of the planet is the inner core, which is the hottest place on Earth. The inner core is a solid ball made of iron and nickel metals, and the temperature inside reaches a scorching 9,900°F! Surrounding this is the outer core, which is liquid but also made of iron and nickel. The next, and widest section, is the mantle, which contains **semi-molten** rock.

The outermost layer is the protective crust. This is the solid rock that all life on Earth lives upon. The crust is divided into big chunks that float around on the mantle. These sections are constantly moving, although it happens so slowly that humans usually can't feel it. However, occasionally two plates will rub against one another causing an earthquake, and if the movement is big enough then people will certainly notice that!

Rocks all begin their lives in different ways, but nearly all of them have one thing in common—they are all made of minerals. A mineral is a naturally occurring, inorganic

solid. That may sound like complicated geology language, but when broken down, it is easier to understand. "Naturally occurring" means that it is not made by humans, and "inorganic" means that it is not alive and isn't made from animal or plant materials. Minerals are made from chemicals and they grow in crystals, just like this piece of rose quartz.

Rose quartz

Rocks can be split into three specific categories: igneous, sedimentary, and metamorphic. The rocks in each group share certain qualities that help define them.

Igneous rocks are created by molten rock called magma that has bubbled up through the mantle layer and hardened. If the magma hardens under the surface of the Earth it forms intrusive igneous rock. If the magma breaks through the mantle and cools on the surface of the Earth, it forms extrusive igneous rock. Pumice, pictured to the right, is an example of extrusive igneous rock.

Sedimentary rock is created by natural materials, such as small parts of other rocks or animal skeletons. Rocks on the surface of the Earth get chipped down to tiny pieces by the wind and rain, and blown or washed away. Over millions of years, the rock parts settle on top of each other and build up in layers. Then they are squashed and compacted together to form new rock.

As rocks get older they evolve and change. Metamorphic rocks begin as either

sedimentary or igneous rocks. If they become exposed to tremendous heat or pressure they undergo a transformation and become metamorphic rocks. Metamorphic rocks are usually very tough because they have been exposed to such extreme conditions.

Pumice

Although they may change, rocks and minerals survive on the Earth for millions of years. Some stay in just one place while others move around in the rivers and oceans.

Scientists have learned vast amounts about the history of the Earth and its inhabitants from rocks, minerals, and fossils. Fossils are the remains, or impressions, of past animals and plants. When an animal dies and its body is quickly buried, its remains are often preserved. The flesh and soft tissue are broken down, leaving just the skeleton behind. The skeleton is then buried in sediment, and layers gradually build up over time. As the skeleton becomes entombed, the layers are squashed down to form sedimentary rock. The bones slowly dissolve and become replaced by minerals from the stone surrounding it. These new minerals form fossils in the shape of the skeleton and will remain hidden until they become exposed and are dug up by a geologist. By digging up fossils, scientists learned that dinosaurs, and other species that are no longer alive today, roamed the Earth more than 100 million years ago!

Becoming a geologist is not for the faint hearted because it will often take people to the darkest and most dangerous depths of the Earth. Geologists need to be determined, and ready to tackle anything that is thrown their way. Not even volcanoes, floods, or earthquakes can keep geologists from finding their next great discovery!

Halite

Geologists know how to look very closely at the world around them—what may look like just a pile of rocks to you or me is a treasure trove of mystery to a geologist.

Rocks, minerals, and fossils come in all shapes and sizes: some big and some small; some rough and some smooth; some dull and others shiny and sparkling! But each and every one tells us lots about how our Earth has evolved over time.

Each type of rock has its own characteristics, and is just waiting for a mineral-minded, rubble-raider to pick it up and decipher the codes within it. The world is full of stony stories and mineral memoirs and there are many reasons why geology rocks!

Geological Timeline

The Earth is approximately 4.5 billion years old. Geologists have been able to date our planet by looking at the type and depth of the rock layers.

mya = millions of years ago

Precambrian
(4,500–550 mya)
Simple plants and animals evolve. Ancient zircon crystals that date back to this era have been discovered in Australia.

Devonian (480–362 mya)
Also known as the Age of the Fishes. Many fossils can be found in the sandstone, limestone, and slate that formed during this period.

Jurassic
(195–141 mya)
Large dinosaurs roamed the land. Rock sediment found in the deep sea was formed during this period.

Permian
(290–248 mya)
Large areas of desert cover the land. One of the world's oldest mountain ranges, the Ural Mountains in Russia, was formed during this period.

Carboniferous
(362–290 mya)
During this period plants thrived and when they died, they fell into the water and were compressed. This created much of the coal that we use today.

Quaternary (2 mya)
Humans appear on the plains of Africa and use rocks as tools to help them hunt and build.

Rock or Mineral?

Mineral

A mineral is a solid that forms naturally—not made by humans. Most minerals are made from two or more chemical elements, such as carbon, oxygen, and calcium to make calcite. Some minerals take thousands of years to form, others take just minutes.

Quartz
Quartz is a common mineral but comes in many different colors—some of these are valued as semiprecious gems.

Feldspar
Feldspars are common minerals and make up 60% of the Earth's crust.

Rock

Rocks are made up of minerals. Different amounts of minerals make different rocks. The different minerals can be clearly seen in some rocks, but a microscope is needed to see them in others.

Granite
This piece of granite is made up of three different minerals. If you look closely you will be able to see the individual crystals within it.

Mica
Some types of mica splits into thin, clear sheets and were once used as window panes.

The Rock Cycle

Rocks are constantly being formed and changed in a process called the rock cycle. Rocks that have been broken down are carried out to the sea, where they are pushed down to form new sedimentary rocks. These in turn are melted and then cooled to form igneous rocks that are eroded by the weather and returned to the sea.

Transportation
Sediment is transported by water, wind, and ice.

Sedimentation
Rocks are carried into the water and fall in layers.

Sedimentary rock
This is formed when the layers of rock are squashed together.

Metamorphic rock
This is formed when sedimentary rocks are heated without melting.

Earth started its life as a huge ball of molten rock. Around 4 billion years ago, the outer layer cooled and formed a hard crust. This made life on Earth possible.

Weathering and erosion
Water flow breaks rocks down to form sediment.

Igneous rock
This is formed by the cooling of magma.

Magma
Liquid rock rises from inside the Earth.

19

ROCK

Hall of Fame

Every rock fits into one of three categories: igneous, sedimentary, or metamorphic. Igneous rocks can be divided further into intrusive and extrusive rocks. Take a look in the Rock Hall of Fame to discover the differences between each group.

IGNEOUS ROCK

Examples: pegmatite, obsidian, pumice.

How the rock formed: by the cooling of magma. Some formed inside the Earth and some outside.
Rock style: large crystals from slow cooling inside the Earth, or small crystals or glassy appearance if cooled on the surface.

METAMORPHIC ROCK

Examples: marble, quartzite, migmatite, schist.

How the rock formed: when rocks were buried under the Earth's crust, high pressures and temperatures caused them to change, forming metamorphic rock.
Rock style: often with small grains formed in straight lines.

SEDIMENTARY ROCK

Examples: limestone, chalk, peat, flint, sandstone.

How the rock formed: when small rocks that had broken away from larger rocks were squashed down and fused together.
Rock style: many-layered and containing lots of different types of rock, fossil, and plant debris.

CHAPTER 2

DISAPPEARING ACT

Depending on how they are formed, some rocks and minerals are strong and durable, but others are weak and crumbly. Many soft rocks can disintegrate in a person's hands if they are squeezed too tightly, so they need to be handled with care.

Geologists have a scale that they use to measure the hardness of minerals: it is called the Mohs scale. The Mohs scale was created by **mineralogist** Friedrich Mohs in 1812 and measures how hard a mineral is, based on how easily it can be scratched.

Geological journal
Rock descriptions

Halite: lavender rock, light purple with white specks. Sparkly!

Talc: dark-green rock, bluish bits; fine coat of white powder. Hands feel greasy.

Graphite: black rock, shiny; sooty marks left on fingers.

Chalk: white rock, crumbly.

Mohs scale ranks minerals on a scale of 1 to 10, the higher the number, the harder the mineral. The hardest known mineral is diamond, so this is ranked at number 10 on the scale. Every mineral can scratch the ones ranked lower down the scale and can be scratched by the ones with a higher number.

Talc

At the opposite end of the scale from diamond, on the softer side of things, is talc. Talc is also a mineral but, unlike diamond, it is so soft that it can be scratched by a human fingernail. Talc is such a delicate material that it is ground down to make talcum powder, which is what babies often smell of. If it is used to absorb moisture from the delicate skin of babies, it must be a big softie!

Talc is one of the many rocks and minerals that is used in daily human life—it is surprising how many can be found around the home. Talc is an important ingredient in many things, such as paint, paper, plastics,

and rubber. Soapstone, which is a form of talc, is also widely used to carve sculptures, bowls, and many other objects. Soapstone was named for the way that it leaves a soapy residue on skin if it is touched. It is perfect for carving because it is easy to scratch, but hard enough not to break.

Another soft rock that you might recognize is chalk. Chalk is a sedimentary rock and is a type of limestone. Natural chalk, or calcite, was used by humans for writing on blackboards.

Chalk

Chalk is made of dead shellfish. The shells from tiny sea creatures settle in the ocean and build up to form layers of rock. Most of them are too tiny to see with the naked eye, but if you look at chalk through a microscope you will be able to see all the individual shell parts. Chalk may look like a dull, white, crumbly piece of rock but in fact it holds a tiny world, filled with the skeletons and shells of millions of creatures.

A vast amount of chalk was formed between 142 and 65 million years ago during the time that dinosaurs roamed the planet. Chalk is often soft, fine-grained, and easily **pulverized**—just the weight of a human hand could be enough to render a chalk stone to dust.

Some people have found that they are allergic to chalk dust. Chalk allergies can cause people to sneeze, much like normal household dust can. If this happens, then the unlucky person may need to make sure they have some tissues available!

Graphite

Another material that is often used in schools is graphite. Graphite is what pencil lead is made from and it takes its name from the Greek word *graphein,* which means "to write." Fine crystals of graphite are very hard to come by—if a geologist finds one it is likely to spark great excitement! The finer crystals of graphite are often in high demand because they are one of the only nonmetallic **conductors** of electricity.

Pencil lead, however is made from the more common form of graphite. Graphite was discovered in England in the 1500s,

when farmers discovered that it was very useful for marking their sheep. People found that they needed to wrap the graphite in string, and later, wood, to stop it from breaking when they were writing with it.

The common name "pencil lead" is slightly misleading because lead is actually a type of metal and is not used to make pencils. When graphite was discovered, people thought that it was a type of metal and so named it *plumbago,* which comes from the Latin for "lead." This name stuck even after people realized that it was actually graphite.

Today, graphite is combined with clay to create different textures of pencil lead— some soft and some hard. This gives artists and writers a wide range of graphite gear to make their marks with.

What misleading name is commonly given to graphite?

Layers of soft sedimentary rock assembles over many years to build everything from small rocks to giant natural structures. Geologists marvel at their intricate patterns and they have been adapted and used for many different everyday jobs. If you look closely, you will discover that sedimentary rocks are all around us, and even more are out there, just waiting to be discovered.

Excerpt from a geologist's diary.

The White Cliffs of Dover, England

Flying over the White Cliffs of Dover is an incredible experience. The cliffs line the English Channel, and looking out over the sea, I can almost see France! The cliffs are made of chalk that has built up over millions of years. They were first formed on the seabed, but over time have become exposed and are now above sea level. The cliffs stay white because they are naturally eroded by the harsh wind and rain that blows in from the channel. This means that the old rocks are constantly being ripped away to reveal the stark, white chalk underneath.

During World Wars I and II, the cliffs were used as a defense for the country. I am reminded of this as I pass by the trenches that dot the area. Rocks sure do have some stories to tell—I can't wait to discover more of them!

Adamantine Auction House

Welcome to the Adamantine Auction House. We specialize in items made from the finest minerals. We have some very rare and exciting items featured today, each made from a different mineral. Get your bidding cards ready!

Lot 1

Antique mercury thermometer

This large, vintage thermometer will add a touch of elegance to any country retreat. The mercury (metallic liquid) inside accurately measures the temperature by increasing and decreasing in size with even the slightest change in conditions.

Quartz watch

This is the perfect timepiece for those who appreciate quality workmanship. Its mechanism is regulated by tiny quartz crystals, which vibrate more than 30,000 times each second, making it a precise timekeeper.

Lot 2

Who would like to start the bidding?

White marble horse statue

This majestic piece dates back to 490BCE. The statue was rescued from the Acropolis in Athens and is made from white marble. The marble has a warm, creamy glow because the crystals inside it reflect light. The statue would be the perfect addition to any home.

Lot 3

Lot 4

Spanish gold coins

These 16th-century coins are made of 22-carat gold and were salvaged from the famous *Nuestra Señora de Atocha* (Our Lady of Atocha) ship, which sank off the coast of Florida in 1622. Gold was often used to make coins because it was flexible and could be pressed into different shapes.

Rock Stars!

Throughout the world, there are natural rock formations that have become famous for their sizes, colors, or cultural meanings. Here are five of the most remarkable rocks on the planet and their locations.

THE GRAND CANYON
Location: Arizona, US
Types of rock: sandstone and limestone
Fact: this enormous gorge was carved by the Colorado River during the last five or six million years.

SHIPROCK
Location: New Mexico, US
Type of rock: volcanic breccia
Fact: it was formed by an explosive volcanic eruption around 30 million years ago.

THE GIANT'S CAUSEWAY
Location: County Antrim, Northern Ireland
Type of rock: basalt
Fact: it is made up of approximately 40,000 interlocking hexagonal columns.

ULURU, OR AYERS ROCK
Location: Northern Territory, Australia
Type of rock: sandstone
Fact: iron-rich minerals on its surface produce its rusty-orange color.

WHITE CLIFFS OF DOVER
Location: Kent, England
Type of rock: chalk
Fact: the cliffs stay white because they are constantly being eroded by wind and rain, so the new layers underneath the surface become exposed.

CHAPTER 3

ODDBALLS AND WEIRDOES

The Earth is a violent and changeable place. Geologists experience this first hand because many of them have to travel to the back of beyond—places with slippery ice, rumbling earthquakes, or explosive volcanoes.

Volcanoes form when the hot, molten rock, which collects in the mantle, can't stand the pressure that builds up beneath it. When this happens, magma breaks through the crust and shoots out of the earth. Volcanoes will form in areas where the crust is particularly weak, and many are situated in an area in the Pacific called The Ring of Fire. This area is a site of great **seismic** activity, which results in earthquakes and volcanoes. The ring is dotted with 75% of the Earth's **active volcanoes** and 90% of all earthquakes occur in this area.

The Earth's movements and eruptions can cause the formation of many different types of rock. The weird and wonderful rocks and minerals that are the products of volcanic outbursts are called igneous rocks and they can come in many shapes and sizes depending on how the magma has cooled. Some volcanic eruptions have been known to destroy whole cities, but geologists brave these areas to dig up information from the depths of the Earth.

One type of rock that is created by magma is pumice. Pumice stones are **porous**, which means that they are filled with thousands of tiny holes, allowing liquid or gas to pass through. When magma erupts from a volcano it is often full of gas, and this makes it burst out of the volcano like soda from a shaken bottle. This lava cools extremely quickly and solidifies into rock.

The thousands of air holes in pumice make it very light, so it can easily float on water and can often be seen flying through the air during a volcanic eruption. In the year 79, Mount Vesuvius, in Pompeii, Italy, erupted. It destroyed the surrounding villages and many people suffocated in the ash clouds that billowed out from the top of the volcano. The villages were buried by up to 65 feet of volcanic material as ash and pumice stones rained down from the sky.

In 1883, the world was rocked by another deadly volcanic eruption. Lava, ash, and rock spewed out of the island of Krakatoa in Indonesia and many people died. After the

Geological journal
Rock descriptions

Pele's hair: hairy rock that looks like a dead rat!

Pumice: pale gray and speckled with craterlike holes. Exceptionally light and rough-feeling.

Fulgurite: looks like a fat tube of pasta covered in sand.

eruption, layers of pumice covered the surrounding ocean. The stones were packed so densely that they reached a depth of almost 5 feet!

Although originating from dangerous sources, pumice has its uses in the home today and is used for polishing and scouring because of its rough surface. It is also commonly used to smooth the skin on people's feet!

Many rocks are so strange looking that they almost seem to be in disguise. Pele's hair, for example, could easily be mistaken for a large, hairy rat.

Pele's hair is an igneous rock that is made of fine, wispy strands of volcanic glass that have rapidly solidified in the air. As it is thrown into the air, the lava is finely spun into strands as thin as human hair. The threads of glass can sometimes reach lengths of 6 feet and can often be blown miles away from the volcano vent that they originated from.

Pele's hair only forms under certain conditions; the air has to be very hot and the lava quite thin or runny. Mount Kilauea in Hawaii provides just such conditions and it was here that this rock was given its name.

Pele is the Hawaiian goddess of fire who is thought to live in the volcano. According to myth, Pele has to be worshipped and respected so that she looks kindly upon the people and the land. However, if anyone disrespects her by stealing rocks from around the volcano she will curse the land by

shooting fire and lava out of the volcano until the rocks are returned to her.

Chunks of Pele's hair not only tell great stories about the Earth and the destructive volcanoes on it, but also about the local cultures of Hawaii. For the Hawaiian people, it remains a warning—do not upset the gods or misfortune may come your way!

Pele's hair

On a stormy day, you will be likely to see silver bolts of light darting through the clouds and reaching toward the Earth, followed by the rumble and boom of thunder. Natural storms can be destructive, breaking rocks down to tiny pebbles, but they can also be creative—transforming rocks into completely new shapes.

If lightning strikes an area of sand, the heat and force of the lightning will **vaporize** it. This causes the sand to fuse together to create a glassy rock formation covered in gritty particles, called fulgurite. Some say that lightning never strikes the same place twice, but often there will be numerous pieces of fulgurite found in one area. The largest fulgurite ever recorded was a towering 16 feet long and was found by geologists in Florida.

Fulgurite maps the course that the lightning takes through the ground and preserves it in a delicate treelike shape. In order to find fulgurite, geologists simply head to the beach and start digging!

Fulgurite

Where was the biggest piece of fulgurite found?

Volcanoes are fascinating and dangerous landforms, and the rocks that spew out of them are a great addition to any geologists' collection. Sometimes, geologists can find amazing rocks just around the corner, but other times rocks and minerals from farther afield might steal their thunder!

Excerpt from a geologist's diary.

Mount Kilauea, Hawaii

Aloha!

For the love of lava, Hawaii has five active volcanoes! I flew over Mt. Kilauea today and it bubbled like a pan of tomato soup!

Kilauea is an active volcano that has been erupting continuously since 1983. So I had better watch out! I stopped off in Hawaii and managed to bag myself some Pele's hair and also a few Pele's tears! The Pele's tears were attached to the strands at the end of the piece of Pele's hair. They are glass particles in teardrop shapes. I had better make sure that the fire goddess, Pele, doesn't find out that I have them, otherwise I will be in big trouble!

Now that I have seen the amazing volcanoes in Hawaii I am going to get back into my plane and continue my trip. I hope to find many more fascinating rocks, minerals, and fossils!

PELE,
THE FIRE GODDESS

Many rocks and minerals are said to have mythological origins. The Hawaiian fire and volcano goddess, Pele, has given her name to two minerals—Pele's hair and Pele's tears. Both are igneous rocks. There are countless stories about Pele. Here is one of them.

Pele was descended from the supreme beings Papa, or Earth Mother, and Wakea, or Sky Father. She is said to be responsible for shaping the islands of Hawaii.

Pursued by her angry sister Na-maka-o-kaha'i, a sea goddess, Pele left her home and became one of the first travelers to Hawaii. She first landed on the island of Kauai. She tried to dig a pit for her home, but every time she dug her stick into the ground to make one, her sister flooded the pit with water and put out Pele's fire.

Pele continued to move down the chain of islands, and finally landed on the Big Island of Hawaii, at Mauna Loa, one of the largest volcanoes on Earth. This mountain was too high, and Na-maka-o-kaha'i could not flood it. Pele had finally found her home. Here, she welcomed her brothers Ka-moho-ali'i, god of sharks; Kane-hekili, who appeared as thunder; Kapoho-i-kahi-ola, who appeared as explosions; Ke-ua-a-kepo, who appeared as showers of fire; and Ke-o-ahi-kama-kaua, who appeared as spears of lava.

To this day, Pele is unpredictable and continues to shape the Hawaiian landscape. When she stamps her feet, she causes earthquakes, and when she digs with her magic stick, she causes eruptions and sends streams of lava down the mountainside of the Kilauea volcano.

This balancing rock in Canada was left on land when the ice glaciers melted. It is perfectly balanced and has defied the powerful forces of nature for centuries.

CHAPTER 4

OUT OF THIS WORLD

Rocks and minerals don't just form under our feet, but also high above our heads. Meteorites are types of rock that are born in space and are sometimes flung through the darkness and into the Earth's atmosphere. Approximately 19,000 meteorites fall to the Earth each year, but most fall into the sea or on deserts. Only four or five specimens are recovered annually, so when they are found they will often send geologists into a spin!

Meteorites are not formed on Earth so have different properties from sedimentary, igneous, and metamorphic rocks. There are three different types of meteorites: irons, which are made of metallic iron and nickel; stony-irons, which are a mixture of irons and stone; and stony meteorites, which are rocks that would have once formed part of the outer crust of a planet or asteroid.

Identifying meteorites is a very difficult science so geologists really have to get their thoughts into orbit. Some meteorites that find their way to Earth are thought to be older than our planet! Many of them are not just a long way from home but may also have been traveling through the cosmos for millions of Earth years!

Since Neil Armstrong became the first person to walk on the moon in 1969, we have learned a great deal about our Earth, the solar system, and the wider universe. Scientists and sharp-eyed geologists have been able to make informed guesses about where they think meteorites may have come from. Some meteorites match the material that has been found on the moon, and others are thought to be chunks of rock that have broken off the red planet, Mars.

The vast majority of meteorites are thought to be fragments of asteroids. Asteroids are made of rock and metal, however they are much larger and can reach lengths of hundreds of miles. Asteroids are formed by space rubble that is left over from the formation of planets and many of them are found in the asteroid belt between Mars and Jupiter.

Many meteorites that enter the Earth's atmosphere are not strong enough to make it to the surface. Meteorites travel through space at incredibly fast speeds and when they are propelled through the Earth's atmosphere they will burn up as they hit the air. These hunks of rock with flaming tails produce, what many people call, shooting stars.

Excerpt from a geologist's diary.

Nullarbour Plain, Australia

G'day!
I've just been to Australia, where I crossed the Nullarbor Plain on a camel. I think a kangaroo ride would have been less bumpy!
As we trundled along the 680-mile desert track, I figured out that "Nullarbor" means "no tree" in Latin. The lack of trees helped me solve that brain-boggler! However, one positively delightful thing I discovered was a glittering chunk of meteorite—yes, meteorite!
Oh, how the iron shimmered in that beating hot sun! I uncovered it while stopping for a glass of lemonade in Premier Downs. There, in the lonely

Outback, meteorites
have landed and because of
the dry climate, have been perfectly
preserved. I think the meteorite that I
have found is a stony-iron meteorite
because of the way that it has a
metallic sheen but also rocky patches
scattered over its surface. However,
I shall take it back to the lab for
further analysis. What a great
find to add to my
collection—I really have
had an out-of-this-
world experience
Down Under!

Iron meteorites are composed mostly of metallic iron and up to 25% nickel—that's some serious heavy metal! This type of meteorite is recognized by scientists because it looks very different from Earth rocks. These extraterrestrial specimens are a wonder to behold because their surface is covered in a pattern called the Widmanstätten Pattern.

This is what is created when iron and nickel crystals merge and cool. The cooling period is so slow that the pattern can take millions of years to form.

Iron is a tough material so iron meteorites are more likely to survive the fall to Earth than stony meteorites—roughly every five out of 100 meteorites that make the journey to the Earth are iron. Meteorites look different from normal rocks because their entry through the atmosphere smooths their edges; the intense heat causes them to melt and often become shiny. One of the best places to search for meteorites is in Antarctica. Ninety percent of all meteorites are found in the southern snowy continent because the cold, dry weather preserves them well and they are easy to spot on the ice and snow.

Tektite

When meteorites plummet to Earth, they can travel at speeds of up to 43 miles per second. When they hit the surface, meteorites can change the shape of the Earth's crust and the surrounding rocks.

The force with which meteorites strike the Earth can throw other rocks and debris up into the air. This pressure melts the rocks and they cool quickly as they bounce and jump. This turns them to glass and forms rocks called tektites.

The Earth is **pockmarked** with impact craters, made by the brutal force of meteorites. These are large holes in the ground that are made by an explosion or

large object falling from the sky. The largest crater that was made by a falling space object is in Vredefort, South Africa, and was thought to be 186 miles wide when it was gouged out of the Earth by an asteroid. Another large crater can be found in Arizona. The Barringer Crater is well preserved because it is so young—in planet years it is only a baby at 50,000 years old!

Although our Earth has to withstand constant attack from space rocks and debris, it is a remarkably hardy planet. Wind, water, and the moving crust help heal the wounds made by meteorites, covering the craters up or wearing them away. Space rocks that plummet to Earth give us an insight into what might be lurking in the cosmos. Who knows what secrets might fall down through our atmosphere in the future!

> How is a tektite different from meteorites?

The Great Beyond: Is There Life Out There?

Name: meteorite Alan Hills 84001 (ALH84001)

Age: approximately 4.5 billion years old

Size: 3½ in. (9 cm) across

Date found: December 27, 1984

Location found: Alan Hills Ice Field, Antarctica

Introduction:

Found on an annual Antarctic expedition in 1984, meteorite ALH84001 has divided the opinions of scientists and caused many to believe that there really could have been life on Mars.

Background:

The meteorite displayed small pockets of gas that matched the atmosphere of Mars perfectly. Scientists found rod-shaped **tubules** within the meteorite that some took to be the fossils of bacteria that had been living on the red planet. This would mean there had been life on Mars. Others believed that these tubules were merely the product of minerals forming at high temperature and so did not support this theory.

Conclusion:

The meteorite is currently being preserved for study at the Johnson Space Center in Houston, Texas. Scientists have still not reached a definite conclusion on whether the meteorite is evidence of life on Mars.

Question:

Do you believe there could be life on Mars?

ENCYCLOPEDIA

Popular topics   Quizzes   Galleries   Lists

Crystals

Article   Websites   Bibliography   Related content

A **crystal** is a solid chemical with a regular, geometrical shape. Crystals typically have smooth, flat faces that meet in sharp edges. They often look shiny or glassy. They form amazing shapes because their atoms and molecules are bonded together in an orderly, regular, repeated pattern. Crystals aren't just flashy gems. Everyday things, such as sugar and salt, are also crystals.

All minerals are made of crystals. This is shown on the outside of the mineral as flat faces arranged in geometric forms. In many rocks, the crystals are too small to see, even with a powerful microscope, but they are there by the thousands. In rare cases, crystals may grow as large as telephone poles.

Twin crystals

Occasionally, crystals may develop in such a way that two (or sometimes more) individual crystals appear to cross each other in a symmetrical manner. Related crystals like this are known as "**twin crystals**."

GEOLOGICA

Crystal symmetry

Crystals can be grouped into seven systems, according to symmetry: **cubic, monoclinic, triclinic, trigonal, hexagonal, orthorhombic**, and **tetragonal**. This is seen in certain regular features of the crystal. For example, for every face, there may be another on the opposite side of the crystal that is similar. However, in most mineral specimens, it may be difficult to determine the symmetry because crystals form gradually and do not have well-developed faces.

Gallery

Tetragonal

Cubic

Trigonal

Hexagonal

Triclinic

Orthorhombic

Monoclinic

A Mineral Mystery

Solving a mineral mystery is never easy, but gathering clues about a mineral's physical properties can help. See if you can match each set of clues to its mineral suspect.

THE SUSPECTS

ORPIMENT

HEMATITE

BARYTE

THE CLUES

EXHIBIT A

habit: has tablelike or four-sided crystals
luster: glasslike, honeylike, or pearly
hardness: 3–3½
streak: white

EXHIBIT B

habit: has grapelike shapes or tablelike crystals
luster: metallic to dull
hardness: 5–6
streak: cherry-red or red-brown

DATA

habit—a mineral's general shape
luster—how shiny a mineral is
hardness—how easily a mineral scratches;
it is measured on a scale from 1 (least hard)
to 10 (hardest) called the Mohs Scale
streak—the color of the powder left behind
after a mineral is dragged across a rough tile

GOLD

EXHIBIT C

habit: 8-sided, 12-sided,
or treelike crystals
luster: metallic
hardness: 2½–3
streak: golden-yellow

EXHIBIT D

habit: no definable shape or
has many leaflike crystals
luster: greasy or honeylike
hardness: 1½–2
streak: pale yellow

ANSWERS: **A.** baryte; **B.** hematite; **C.** gold; **D.** orpiment

CHAPTER 5

NOW YOU SEE IT

Some minerals are deceptive and can lull geologists into a false sense of security. Sometimes geologists need a bit of help to shed some light on the true identity of the minerals that they have found.

The misleading minerals in question all have the ability to glow different colors when they are put underneath an ultraviolet (UV) light. UV light is a type of light that is not visible to the naked human eye. The sun sends out UV light, which in large doses can be harmful to humans and causes sunburn. Concentrated UV light can make some rocks glow and light up like Christmas trees.

Glow-in-the-dark minerals appear pretty average in normal daylight. However, if you take them into a dark place and shine a UV light on them, they instantly transform into stunning and colorful specimens. Once the UV light is turned off they will return back to their original states. Now you see the minerals, and now you don't!

Calcite, autunite, and scheelite are examples of these types of glowing rocks and are described as having "excited atoms." The atoms inside them take in light, get energized, and then appear to glow. This is called **fluorescence**.

Calcite is a very common mineral, which grows anywhere that water will reach. It forms a variety of spectacular crystals and in its purest form is called marble. Inside caves, calcite forms long, thin stalactites that build up as water drips down from the ceiling.

Excerpt from a geologist's diary.

Waitomo, New Zealand

Isn't New Zealand fun? I came here to find some magnificent minerals and I have ended up learning how to hula dance and ski on a volcano! Mount Ruapehu has bubbling mud pools and spouting geysers, which shoot steam straight out of holes in the ground!

I paddled a canoe into the Waitomo cave and was lucky enough to see quite a show. The cave walls were twinkling, just like the stars in the night sky. I thought I had found some phosphorescent rocks for my wonderful collection. My tour guide chuckled when I told her and she had to set me straight—the glowing walls weren't phosphorescent rocks, they were glow worms!

Scheelite, adamite, and calcite are all rocks that fluoresce. When a UV light is shone on them, they will gleam a bright color. Once the UV light is turned off, the bright colors will fade and the rocks will return to their stony disguises. Willemite works slightly differently, and once the UV light is turned off, it will continue to shine and glow. Some rocks that contain willemite are phosphorescent and have an afterglow when the light is removed.

Phosphorescent willemite is quite a rare find. Large reserves of it can be found in Franklin, New Jersey, along with many other rare minerals. Willemite can also be found in the Netherlands, which is where it was given

Adamite

Scheelite

its name. The mineral was named after the king who reigned from 1772–1843, King Willem I.

The rechargeable power of willemite causes it to glow a bright green color when under UV light and to continue glowing after the light source is removed. This is similar to the glow-in-the-dark stars that you can buy to stick on your ceiling. One minute they look like plain white shapes, but turn off the light and you have a whole universe twinkling down at you.

Willemite

Calcite

Scheelite is a fluorescent mineral that is very important because it is a rich source of tungsten. Tungsten is an **element** that is used to make tungsten metal. Tungsten has the highest melting point of all the metallic elements. Being able to withstand tremendous heat means that tungsten is the perfect material for making drill bits and electric light bulb **filaments**.

The nose of the Saturn V rocket was made from tungsten because the metal can cope with the blistering temperatures as it is propelled through the Earth's atmosphere. Saturn V was the American rocket that launched the Apollo 11 mission capsule, which landed the first people on the moon in 1969.

Scheelite

Adamite

Although they have many useful properties, minerals are not perfect and will often have impurities. Impurities are foreign elements that have infiltrated a mineral's structure and are often responsible for the mineral's color. The foreign elements that often show up in adamite minerals are: copper, which gives the mineral a vibrant green or yellow color, or manganese, which makes adamite appear pink or purple.

Another mineral that geologists often search for is autunite. Autunite is a fluorescent mineral that has an attractive yellow–green sheen, but geologists beware, this mineral can be dangerous!

Autunite contains the element uranium, which is naturally radioactive. Radioactivity can have bad effects on the human body if it is exposed to it for a long period of time. For example, **radiation** can cause people to lose their hair and it can affect the cells within the blood, brain, and heart.

Never fear though, geologists know how to protect themselves and although they can't help but gaze at a beautiful piece of

Calcite

Willemite

autunite, they will be sure to keep it stored away and handled as little as possible. If kept in an airtight container, radon, a radioactive gas, can build up around the mineral so proper ventilation is needed before opening the box.

Fluorescent minerals can glow and sparkle when under UV light. Other minerals sparkle permanently; these are called gemstones and are often bought and sold for very high prices.

Why does autunite need to be stored carefully?

The structure of Minerals

Minerals are made up of elements. Elements are made up of tiny particles called atoms. These atoms can stick together in different ways to form different minerals.

The atom

The atom of each element is unique to that element because it has a specific number of protons. Protons are parts that have a positive electrical charge. Atoms are also made up of negatively charged parts called electrons and parts with no charge called neutrons.

Nucleus is made up of neutrons and protons.

Number of protons and electrons is the same.

Electrons orbit the nucleus.

Molecules

Atoms can bond or join up with other atoms of the same element or of a different element to form molecules.

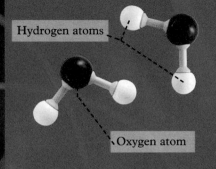

Hydrogen atoms

Oxygen atom

These two elements combine to form water.

Allotropes

Sometimes two different sets of molecules of the same atoms can form different minerals. These are called allotropes and occur because the atoms can be bonded together in different ways. The atoms of the element carbon, for example, can bond to form diamonds or graphite (pencil lead).

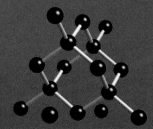

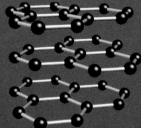

Atoms in diamonds are strongly bonded to four others to form a stiff, compact structure.

Carbon atoms in graphite are closely linked to three others arranged in widely spaced layers that are only weakly bonded together.

ULTRAVIOLET DISCO

Fluorescence or phosphorescence?

Many minerals fluoresce. This means that they glow when under a UV lamp, but they stop glowing once the lamp is turned off. Other minerals are phosphorescent. This means that they continue to glow after the UV lamp has been turned off because they release their light at a slower rate.

Get your atoms excited at the Ultraviolet Disco!

Come and glow the night away to some rocking tunes and stone-cold beats. The Ultraviolet Disco has been named the mineral hangout of the year and is guaranteed to get all your atoms jumping!

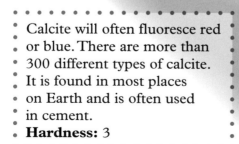

Calcite will often fluoresce red or blue. There are more than 300 different types of calcite. It is found in most places on Earth and is often used in cement.
Hardness: 3

Calcite

78

Adamite fluoresces bright green. It forms in great quantities in the Ojuela Mine in Mexico, among other places on Earth.
Hardness: 3.5

Adamite

Willemite

Willemite often fluoresces green and was used in the tubes of early televisions.
Hardness: 5.5

What's happening?

The atoms of these rocks absorb energy from the ultraviolet light and become "excited." They stay in this excited state for no more than tiny fractions of a second; then, as they move back into their "unexcited" state, termed their "ground" state, the energy they absorbed is released as fluorescent light.

RADIOACTIVITY

Some elements are naturally radioactive. Radioactivity at a low level is a natural part of the world around us, and is harmless. It is found in some kinds of rocks and even some foods. A few rocks and minerals have higher levels: always ask an adult to help you with them.

**RADIOACTIVITY DESTROYS LIVES.
LOOK OUT FOR THIS SYMBOL.**

META-TORBERNITE

URANINITE

AUTUNITE   **CARNOTITE**

HANDLE RADIOACTIVE SPECIMENS WITH CARE.

⚠ Store potentially radioactive specimens in airtight containers in a garage or basement.

⚠ Avoid direct contact with radioactive specimens.

⚠ Never eat, drink, or sleep near any radioactive specimens.

⚠ Label all radioactive specimens as radioactive.

WHAT IS RADIOACTIVITY?

Most atoms have stable nuclei—the number of neutrons and protons in the nucleus stays the same. Others, such as uranium atoms, have unequal numbers of neutrons and protons. This makes them unstable and likely to break down, or decay. When an unstable atom decays, it releases energy called radiation. In large doses, radiation is extremely dangerous to a person's health. In small doses, it can be used to fight cancer and to take x-rays.

This underground cave, or cenote, in Mexico, was formed when the limestone rock collapsed, exposing a secret pool of water below.

CHAPTER 6

THE LADIES

Precious stones have a rich and colorful history and have been objects of desire for thousands of years. In the past, gems have been used as weapons as well as to add sparkle and glamour to jewelry. All manner of "jewels," from humble seashells to extraordinary emeralds, have been found in graves dating back 20,000 years. Many ancient cultures believed that people's souls went to an afterlife when they died. This meant that they buried people with items

such as bowls, clothes, and jewelry that they thought might be useful in the next life.

Gemstones are chosen for their beauty, which is defined by their color and the way that they reflect light. Gemstones also have to be rare and durable, and are either minerals or organics, which have been made by plants or animals.

Like rocks, gemstones are created by the geological processes that create, shape, and reshape the Earth. Heat and pressure are the main factors that create gemstones within the Earth. Many stones are brought to the surface by volcanic eruptions, but others are found in rocks or in gem gravels, which are fragments left by rivers or streams as they gradually erode rocks. The gems will then be discovered by geologists and miners who sell them to others to be cut and polished.

Amber

Pearls are organic gems that come in all shapes and sizes. They grow inside oysters and mussels and are a defense mechanism, designed to protect the mollusk from intruding particles. When an **irritant**, such as a grain of sand, enters the shell, the mollusk releases layers of calcium carbonate, or "nacre," which build up around the particle. This forms a pearl.

Up until the 1900s, pearls were reserved for those who had lots of money. They were so scarce and expensive that no one else could afford them. Recognizing this demand, a Japanese **entrepreneur** learned how to encourage oysters to make pearls. This was done by inserting an irritant into the oyster, rather than waiting for one to find its way there naturally. This meant that pearls could be grown in abundance, and also that they were similar in size and shape.

Stories of pearls have been in myths and legends for many centuries. Pearls were probably first discovered by ancient people when they were searching the seas for food,

and they are still often called "fruits of the sea." In past centuries, pearls were thought to be tears of the gods and they have even been used as medicines to cure everything from fevers to stomach ulcers. Even today, powdered pearl is used in China to create creams that treat skin conditions.

Organic gems are softer than mineral gems but are no less valuable. People trawl the seas for the perfect natural pearl, hoping to find its lustrous, shimmering surface on the ocean floor.

Pearl

Another gemstone that falls in the organic category is amber. Amber is the product of tree resin that hardens and forms golden **globules**, which become preserved for many years. Most pieces of amber date back to approximately 30–50 million years ago but some are even older and solidified at a time when dinosaurs walked the Earth.

The resin that drips down a tree when its bark has been punctured is sweet-smelling, and many small creatures are lured in by the hope of snatching a tasty morsel. Unfortunately, once they have been tempted nearer, the creatures are not always able to move out of the stream of sticky resin quickly enough. Insects, scorpions, lizards, and frogs have been found encased in amber and caught in the act of trying to sip some sap from the tree. These creatures stuck in suspended animation help **paleontologists** reconstruct life from lost worlds—more than 1,000 extinct species have been identified this way.

Like most other gems that are in high demand, fake versions created out of plastic have been sold by people as real amber. Some pretend specimens look so realistic that even scientists from the Natural History Museum in London, England, were fooled by an **ersatz** piece of fossilized amber!

Exerpt from a geologist's diary.

Tahiti, French Polynesia

Ia Orana! (That's Tahitian for "hello"!) I've traveled to Tahiti to go diving for some pearls. I heard they have the most beautiful ones here!

As soon as I reached the island, I dipped straight in the Bora Bora lagoon with my diving instructor, Poema. I have flown over some exquisite waters, but Bora Bora really was the cream on the cake! I almost forgot my terror of being chomped by a shark or zapped by a stingray.

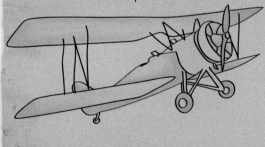

I did see a manta ray,
and it was majestic!
In this underwater
wonderland, I gathered
black oyster shells in
my net. Later on the beach, Poema and I pried open
the shells. Yes, we had a hearty feast of oysters! In
one shell, like a little globe of midnight,
sat a magnificent black
Tahitian pearl. I named
my pearl after Poema
(which means
"deep-sea pearl").

Many people devote their lives to finding and selling rare gemstones. The wonder and excitement, and the potential money that can be made, keeps people searching to the ends of the Earth.

Different techniques are used to extract gemstones from the earth and rocks burying them. Some can be as easy as panning for stones in a riverbed, while others involve the use of costly mining equipment.

Diamonds are often found in Africa, both in the oceans surrounding the continent and on land. Diamond mining is a large-scale operation and over 275 tons of rock have to be blasted away for every one diamond carat, or 200 milligrams, extracted!

Rubies however are panned for, using an age-old method. Workers sift gravel from riverbeds and pick the gems out by hand.

Once they have been found, gems need to be cut and polished to transform them into jewels. Cutting gems allows light to pass through the stone and be reflected back

Ruby

from its many surfaces. This makes the gem sparkle and shimmer.

Throughout time, wars have been waged and honor challenged to gain possession of countless beautiful gemstones. Some are believed to be cursed, whereas others are thought to bring good fortune. Most of them will remain priceless and **coveted** by humans from all over the world, willing to risk their lives to find the most exquisite specimens.

PEARLS

Pearls are precious gems, which are often sold at a high price, but what is their purpose and how are they produced?

Formation

Pearls are most commonly found growing inside the shells of oysters. They are formed when a small particle, which might be harmful to the oyster, gets into the shell and becomes stuck in the mantle.

Process

1. A particle of grit finds its way into the oyster's shell.

2. The mantle (protective layer that covers the oyster's organs) releases minerals that form nacre, or mother of pearl. The nacre covers the invading particle.

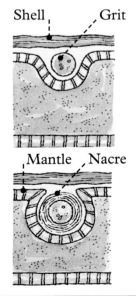

3. The layers of nacre build up in a sphere shape around the grit to form a pearl. The pearl comes free keeping the oyster safe from harm.

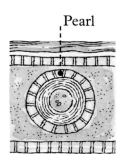

Pearl

Farming
To meet demand, oyster farms are needed to produce pearls quickly. It can take up to four years for a farmed pearl to fully develop. Farmers plant a tiny sphere of mother of pearl into the oyster and then place it back into the sea. The oyster will then form a pearl around the sphere.

Finery
Many people place a great value on pearls. They are used to decorate jewelry and ornaments and are valued by their color, shape, and texture.

Amazing Amber

Amber is known as an organic gem. It is not made from minerals but from a plant. Coniferous trees release a sticky substance called resin when their bark is punctured. The resin oozes out of the tree and covers the damaged area of the bark. This hardens as it dries. Over millions of years, the resin becomes fossilized to form amber.

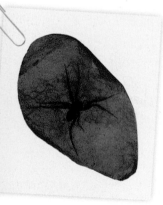

Preserved pests
Insects and spiders often become trapped in tree resin. As the resin dries and fossilizes, the dead creatures are preserved in the dried amber. Scientists have found amber with creatures inside dating from 40–60 million years ago.

Electrifying elements
The word for "electricity" comes from the Greek name for amber—electrum. Ancient Greek scientists noticed that amber had an electric charge when rubbed. This charge is called static.

Golden Gems

Amber is a popular gem to be used for jewelry because of its golden-orange color.

The Amber Room in Catherine Palace, Russia
Made in 1711, the amber wall panels mysteriously disappeared in World War II. The room was rebuilt in 2003.

GEMSTONES AND BIRTHSTONES

From sparkling diamonds to rich red rubies, some rocks are valuable and are known as gems. They are mined from the Earth at huge expense, cut and polished, and worked into jewelry. Some people believe it is lucky to wear gems that are linked to their months of birth. Which is your birthstone?

JANUARY—Garnet

FEBRUARY—Amethyst

MARCH—Aquamarine

APRIL—Diamond

MAY—Emerald

JUNE—Pearl

JULY—Ruby

AUGUST—Peridot

SEPTEMBER—Sapphire

OCTOBER—Opal

NOVEMBER—Topaz

DECEMBER—Turquoise

GEM CUTS

Gemstones have a rough and dull surface when they are first extracted from the Earth. In order to get them into a sparkling and elegant shape, they need to be cut and polished. There are four types of precious stones: diamonds, rubies, sapphires, and emeralds. All the others are called semiprecious.

People who cut and polish gems are called lapidaries.

POPULAR GEM CUTS

Table cut

Pear brilliant

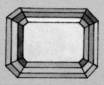

Round brilliant

Cabochon

Rose cut

Emerald or step cut

FACETING

The best way to boost the beauty of a transparent (see-through) gem is to cut the surface into a number of facets or faces. This is done by grinding the gem down with a rotating wheel.

A piece of rough diamond with eight sides is selected.

The point at the top is sawn off to form a top facet.

The stone is rounded and the top is cut.

Pairs of facets are cut on the top.

The smaller facets are cut.

The diamond is rotated and the bottom facets cut.

The finished brilliant cut highlights the colors of the stone, making it twinkle.

CHAPTER 7

ROCKING AND ROLLING

The rocks and minerals described in this book are a small selection of the wide variety that is out there. They are just the tip of the mountain and there are thousands more to discover.

Rocks and minerals can be found everywhere—at home, school, or work, in cities, on the beach, or at the bottom of the ocean. Geologists work hard to understand the Earth and all the wonderful materials that we have within our reach. Geologists

investigate many different things on Earth; not only do they search for stones but some also specialize in other natural resources such as crude oil, gas, and water. Geology is such a varied subject that a geologist can be called upon to examine the ground when a new building is going to be built, assess an area where fossils or meteorites have been found, or help predict when a volcano might erupt. They certainly have plenty to keep them busy!

Coal, crude oil, and gas are known as "fossil fuels." Crude oil and gas originate from dead sea creatures and coal is made from dead plants; they all release energy when they are burned. Most of the electricity in the United States is generated by burning fossil fuels, so they need to be extracted from the Earth in very large quantities.

Oil-bearing rock

Crude oil is formed in the ocean by the **decomposition** of tiny organisms. When they die, their bodies sink to the bottom of the ocean and become buried in mud. Over millions of years the mud turns to rock, which squashes the animal remains and forms oil. The oil moves up through the rock layers by seeping into the pores of the rocks above it.

Extracting oil from rocks is a very difficult and costly process. By looking at the structure of the rocks geologists are able to predict where oil companies might be able to find oil. Oil was formed millions of years ago and because humans have become so dependent upon it, it is being used up at a faster rate than it is created. It is predicted that oil reserves will run out in the next 30 years if it is not used more efficiently. Crude oil is a nonrenewable resource because once the Earth's store of it has run out, there will be none left.

Coal is also a nonrenewable energy source. Coal was created millions of years ago by the decay and burial of plants. This decay forms peat (turf), which is then buried and squashed. Eventually, if the pressure and heat is high enough, this will make coal. The highest-quality coal is anthracite because it contains the highest percentage of carbon, which is an ideal fuel.

Scientists have been trying to find other sources of **renewable** fuel for humans to use. Fossil fuels will not last forever and need to be used sparingly.

Anthracite

Diamond mineral

Another expensive material that is made from carbon is diamond. Diamond is formed deep inside the mantle at depths of approximately 55 miles. When carbon is subjected to crushing pressures and intense heat it transforms into diamond, the hardest mineral on Earth.

Diamonds are pushed up to the surface of the Earth by magma. As the magma rushes past, it will sweep diamonds and other minerals along with it, forcing them up, reaching toward the open air. When the

magma cools it will form carrot-shaped tubes of kimberlite rock. Over millions of years the upper part of the tubes are eroded away, exposing the diamonds inside.

Diamonds are mined from deep pits in the Earth. The deeper the pits descend, the harder the rock becomes, so mining companies have to use explosives to blast away the rock and extract the diamonds.

Most of the Earth's natural diamonds can be found in Africa, but many of the South African mines have already been emptied, due to the high demand for the gem. Diamonds can reach a very high price and they are often sold in order to finance wars. Diamonds sold for this purpose are called "blood diamonds."

What are diamonds made from?

Formed millions of years ago, diamonds are tiny time capsules that can tell scientists about the places deep within the Earth, where humans are unable to visit. Impurities in diamonds cause them to exhibit an array of different colors. Traces of nitrogen in a diamond will cause it to look yellow or brown and if boron is present then it will appear blue. Colored stones are called "fancies," and pink and red ones are the rarest, with only a few of them being found every year.

The value of a diamond jumps up as soon as the rough stone is cut, to reveal the fiery brilliance within it. All diamonds have the potential to be stunning and this is where the phrase "a diamond in the rough" originates from. The phrase means that someone or something has hidden qualities and with a little polishing they, or it, can become exceptional and stand out from the crowd.

When miners discovered the vast South African diamond reserves in the 1870s, diamonds became more plentiful. This meant that prices for the gems went down. This

worried the mining company De Beers because the owner wanted to make as much profit as possible. So they came up with a genius idea to make more people buy their diamonds. De Beers created an advertising campaign that encouraged people to buy diamond engagement rings. Next thing they knew, every American bride-to-be had a dazzling diamond on her finger and diamond sales were booming.

Diamond

Excerpt from a geologist's diary.

Minas Gerais, Brazil

The last stop on my geological jaunt around the world is sunny Brazil. I have come to a diamond mine to see if I can help spot any stunning sparklers.
Brazilian diamonds were discovered in 1725 by gold miners who were working  along the banks of the Jequitinhonha River. Although Brazil is not the biggest producer of diamonds, it is a great place to find rare red and pink ones.

The mine here is a family business and they have all been quick to show me the ropes! As a geologist, I'm always happy to help when I can.

On my second day here, we hit the jackpot and found five rough pink diamonds. They're so beautiful, it's easy to see why they're often called a "girl's best friend."

As the sun beats down in the afternoon, the smell of jasmine wafts over from the nearby fields. I have been told that this comes from the coffee bean plants that are growing nearby.

My last stop before I head home is to the mineral-water springs, for a relaxing dip in the warm water. I think I need a rest after all of this traveling and hard work.

Searching for rocks and minerals can be incredibly rewarding and an amazing way for us to understand our planet. Without the help of geologists we wouldn't know how to predict an earthquake or volcanic eruption, what our planet is made of, or that a *Tyrannosaurus rex* could have grown to 20 feet tall when it was alive. Rocks and minerals tell some fascinating stories and they continue to roll through history, evolving and changing as they go.

People are always digging farther and farther into the Earth, in search of better resources to use. However, we need to remember that we only have one Earth and we need to look after it. We rely upon rocks and minerals to make our lives easier, and they are often working away in the background, without us even noticing.

Why not try to understand all of these hard-working rocks and minerals for yourself by doing your own rubble research or stony studies? See if you can discover the next mysterious mineral or fascinating fossil.

You never know what you might find on this great big rock that we call "home." You might stumble across a glittering jewel, a preserved dinosaur, or even a meteorite from an unknown alien world. Thousand of rocks and minerals are out there, just waiting for you to pick them up and discover the magic within them.

DIAMOND DAZZLERS

Welcome to Heart of Gold Jewelers. Here is our display of the most famous diamonds in the world. Each one has been cut to perfection, and many have been owned by some of the most influential people in history.

Great Star of Africa *(530.2 carats)*
This diamond—cut from the Cullinan Diamond—is the largest cut diamond in the world. It is now on display in the Tower of London in England and mounted in Great Britain's Royal Scepter.

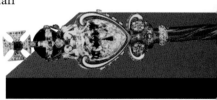

Koh-i-Noor *(105.6 carats)*
Since 1304, this diamond, whose name means "mountain of light," has been owned by many Indian and Persian rulers. The jewel became part of Britain's crown jewels in 1877. It is on display with the Great Star of Africa in the Tower of London, England.

Millennium Star *(203 carats)*
It took three years for experts to cut this diamond—discovered in 1990—into its flawless pear shape. It is so perfect that jewelers still struggle to put a price on it. It is owned by diamond company De Beers.

Hope Diamond *(45.5 carats)*
Some believe that this dark-blue diamond brings misfortune to those who own or wear it. One of its owners was Marie Antoinette, who was beheaded in 1793. It can now be seen at the Smithsonian Museum of Natural History in Washington, DC.

Collecting Rocks

It's easy to find lots of amazing rocks near your home. All you need is a pair of sharp eyes and a bit of patience. Here are some tips to help you get started.

WHAT YOU WILL NEED

- bag for collecting rocks
- water
- large bowl
- detergent
- scrubbing brush
- pocket knife
- magnifying glass

WARNING!

Pocket knives can be dangerous. Only use these with adult supervision.

IMPORTANT!

To be a good rock collector, you need to follow certain safety procedures.

1 Walk slowly as you look at the ground and collect as many different types of rock as you can: hard, soft, smooth, shiny, rough, crumbly, flat, and so on. Don't worry if they are dirty—you can clean them at home.

2 Clean the rocks when you get home. Brush off loose dirt, or scrape it off with a pocket knife. Then wash the rocks in warm water with a little detergent. Use a scrubbing brush to remove dirt.

3 Let the rocks dry, and then inspect them with a magnifying glass. Can you see individual grains or crystals? Feel the rocks carefully to see which ones are hard or crumbly.

TIP

The best places to look for rocks are on cliffs or in quarries, and along beaches, riverbeds, and fields. Cliffs and quarries can be dangerous, though, so go with an adult.

Start a Collection

A collection of rocks grows better and better over time, and the best specimens can be arranged to make a spectacular display. It's important to label all your specimens and keep a careful record of everything you know about them.

WHAT YOU WILL NEED

- your specimens
- white correction fluid, or white stickers
- black fine-point permanent marker
- index cards
- two index card files
- cardboard specimen trays, matchbox trays, or egg cartons
- cotton balls or tissue paper
- magnifying glass

1 Assemble your specimens. Put a small dab of correction fluid on an unimportant side of each one and let it dry. Alternatively, use a small white sticker. Use the permanent marker to write a reference number on each mark or sticker, starting with 1.

Index cards

Magnifying glass

Correction fluid

Cotton balls

2 Fill out an index card for each specimen, writing its number at the top. Write down the type of rock and the name of the mineral or fossil (if you know them) under the number. Also write down where each specimen came from and any other interesting details. Keep the cards in number order.

3 Prepare a second index card with the name of the rock, fossil, or mineral at the top and its number below. Keep these cards in alphabetical order in a separate card file. You can then look up specimens by name and number.

4 Place each specimen in a small cardboard tray, matchbox tray, or egg carton. Put cotton balls or tissue paper under delicate specimens. Arrange your specimen trays in a drawer or large box to display them.

MYSTERY OF GIANT DINOSAUR SOLVED!

Batz Besud—Mongolian correspondent

Paleontologists are astonished to recover the bones of a dinosaur that has been baffling scientists since 1965.

The gigantic arms of the *Deinocheirus mirificus* were unearthed by scientists in the Gobi desert in the 60s, but the rest of the remains were stolen by poachers and were thought to have been sold to private collectors. Since then, scientists have only been able to speculate about what kind of beast the arms might have belonged to.

Scientists have struggled to build a picture of the dinosaur because until now they only had the six-foot-long, clawed arm bones to guide their investigation. In 2009, paleontologists found some more pieces of the puzzle while on another dig in the desert, but the skull, hands, and feet were still missing.

Last week, these previously poached bones were found in a fossil shop in Belgium. Scientists are dumbfounded by the creature that the skeleton has revealed.

The *Deinocheirus mirificus* would have lived approximately 70 million years ago and has been measured at 35 feet long, which is larger than a *Tyrannosaurus rex*. It walked upright on long legs, had a sail-like ridge along its curved back, and a curious, toothless duck bill. The beast is related to a family of dinosaurs that have been described as "ostrichlike," but this one is much larger than any ostrich that is alive today.

Scientists are ecstatic to solve the enigma of the dino-claws and will continue to excavate the rock in the Mongolian desert, hoping to find more new and exciting species.

AWESOME ROCKS QUIZ

See if you can remember the answers to these questions about what you have read.

1. What is the Earth's inner core made of?

2. What type of rock is pumice?

3. What is the name of the scale that is used to measure the hardness of minerals?

4. What are the three types of rock that are formed on Earth?

5. What is the name of the volcano that erupted in Pompeii in the year 79?

6. What word is used to describe how shiny a mineral is?

7. Where on Earth is the best place to find meteorites?

8. What is the term used for when a rock glows under UV light?

9. What mineral is used to regulate watch mechanisms?

10. What is the name of the largest cut diamond in the world?

11. What is the Hawaiian volcano goddess called?

12. Which metal was used to make the nose of the Saturn V rocket?

13. What happens when an unstable atom decays?

14. Why is autunite dangerous?

15. What does "Poema" mean?

Answers on page 125.

GLOSSARY

Conductors
Materials that allow heat or electricity to move through them.

Cosmos
The universe

Coveted
Something that is desired.

Element
Chemical substance that is made of a single type of atom.

Entrepreneur
Person who sets up a business and takes on risks, in the hope of making money.

Ersatz
Artificial

Filaments
Thin wires used in light bulbs that glow when electricity passes through them.

Fluorescence
When a material absorbs light and sends it out, appearing to glow.

Globules
Small balls of something, often a thick liquid.

Irritant
Something that causes discomfort.

Mineralogist
Scientist that studies the properties of minerals and their crystal structure.

Paleontologists
People who study fossils to learn about
how life on Earth has changed.

Pockmarked
Covered in holes.

Porous
Describes an object that has small holes, which allow
gas or liquid to pass through.

Pulverized
Crush something into tiny pieces.

Radiation
Energy that can be dangerous to humans and travels
in invisible waves or rays.

Seismic
Relating to earthquakes or vibrations from the Earth.

Semi-molten
Describes a substance that is between a liquid
and a solid.

Tubules
Small tubes

Vaporize
Turn something into vapor or smoke.

Answers to the Rock Box Quiz:

1. Iron and nickel; **2.** Extrusive igneous; **3.** Mohs scale;
4. Igneous, metamorphic, and sedimentary; **5.** Vesuvius;
6. Luster; **7.** Antarctica; **8.** Fluorescence; **9.** Quartz;
10. Great Star of Africa; **11.** Pele; **12.** Tungsten;
13. It releases energy called radiation; **14.** It contains
uranium, which is radioactive; **15.** Deep-sea pearl.

INDEX

About the Author

Katy Lennon was born and raised in the UK, where she spent a lot of her childhood reading as many books as she could get her hands on. She moved to the seaside town of Brighton to complete her degree and now enjoys being an editor at DK, helping create books for young, inquiring minds. She lives in East London with three housemates and two cats and spends her spare time knitting, watching films, reading, and listening to records on her Dad's old record player.

About the Consultants

Kevin Walsh has been a geology lecturer in Zimbabwe and an assistant curator for rocks and minerals at Oxford University Museum of Natural History. He has studied geology and collected minerals, rocks, and fossils in many parts of the world.

Dr. Linda Gambrell, Distinguished Professor of Education at Clemson University, has served as President of the National Reading Conference, the College Reading Association, and the International Reading Association. She is also reading consultant to the *DK Readers*.

Have you read these other great books from DK?

DK ADVENTURES

Mount Vesuvius erupts in this adventure. Will Carlo escape?

It's a life-or-death adventure as the gang searches for a new home planet.

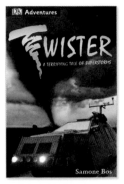

Chase twisters in Tornado Alley in this pulse-racing action adventure.

Experience ancient Roman intrigue in this time-traveling adventure.

Emma adores horses. Will her wish come true at a riding camp?

Lucy follows her dream.... Will she make the cut?